CHRISTIAN,
AWAKE!

DAVID SCRIMSHAW

Xulon
PRESS

Dedicated
to those who
watch and warn!

TABLE OF CONTENTS

INTRODUCTION

Alarm Clocks

Alarm clocks–You probably have more than one, possibly even including that old wind up one that you do not know where it came from! Why do we have them? How do we use them? Why do we not like them?

We have alarm clocks because we must sleep to rest our minds and bodies. If we are very tired or ill, we might not wake up in time to do something important.

I think most of us use them to remind us of an important appointment like making it to work or school on time. We might even use one for cooking so that our food is not burned to a crisp or raw and inedible.

How we use them is interesting. We set the alarm for a certain time to wake us that will allow us to get ready for an appointment. However, there is this funny button on most alarm clocks or alarm radios—the snooze button. I have no idea why you would want to ignore the alarm when it is telling you that you need to get up for something important. However, some alarms even allow you to hit the snooze button over and over again!

Then there is that annoying noise! No one could stay asleep with all that racket which is precisely the idea of an alarm clock. You see, we need warnings that will rouse us from sleep or distractions because we are fallible humans.

This book is a brief look at why we humans, Christians or pre-believers, are in desperate need of a wake-up call. Time is short, just as it is when the alarm clock goes off. We may have time to make it safely to our destination, but there could be something lurking out there like rain or a distracted driver that would make getting to our appointment on time an impossibility.

In this book, we will be considering what God has to say about spiritual sleep, rest, watchfulness, alarms of various kinds, hitting the snooze button, and appointments of the divine nature. It is my hope that this will be a kind of *alarm book* that sets you to thinking about your spiritual relationship with the Creator. I purposely did *not* include a snooze button!

Chapter 1

WAKE UP

And unto the angel of the church in Sardis write; These things saith he that hath the seven Spirits of God, and the seven stars; I know thy works, that thou hast a name that thou livest, and art dead. Be watchful, and strengthen the things which remain, that are ready to die: for I have not found thy works perfect before God. Remember therefore how thou hast received and heard, and hold fast, and repent. If therefore thou shalt not watch, I will come on thee as a thief, and thou shalt not know what hour I will come upon thee. Thou hast a few names even in Sardis which have not defiled their garments; and they shall walk with me in white: for they are worthy. He that overcometh, the same shall be clothed in white

raiment; and I will not blot out his name out of the book of life, but I will confess his name before my Father, and before his angels. He that hath an ear, let him hear what the Spirit saith unto the churches. (Revelation 3:1-6)

My first-born son had been looking forward to my return home from a day at work. I did not spend enough time with him. I was hoping for a quiet week of serving as the duty chaplain at Wright-Patterson AFB so I could really spend some quality time with my son. It was a warm spring Ohio day. Dinner was on the table. We had prayed and began eating a delicious meal of home-made lasagna when the phone rang.

"Chaplain?" asked the voice. "We need you over at the hospital."

"Yes, of course," I answered. "What is the problem?"

"We have had a civilian death in the E.R. The Doc there does not want to tell the wife until you get there" he said.

"I am coming right now," I promised. "Who should I ask for?"

The Duty Officer gave me the doctor's name, I got in my car, and drove the twelve-minute trip to the Medical Center.

When I arrived, I saw a freshly minted Captain who was also a doctor.

He had his back to me as I approached, and I heard him say, "Where is that Chap(lain)?"

He had his garrison cap in one hand, and was repeatedly slapping it into the palm of his other.

"I am right here, doc. Can you fill me in?" I asked.

"I have a civilian who died, well, he was probably dead before we got him in here. He and his wife and a friend were in their pick-up truck, traveling down Kauffman Ave. when he began complaining of severe chest pain. By the time security let them through and we got him in here, he was unresponsive."

Quietly, I asked, "Did you work on him long?"

"We intubated and performed CPR—probably thirty minutes or so. I think I probably broke some of his ribs, but that does not matter now..." his voice faded off. "Well, you got this now, right, Chap?"

"Yes, what was his name and his wife's name?" I asked.

After consulting with the Doctor, I went into the treatment room. They had moved the body on the gurney to a room for privacy. I briefly met and escorted the deceased man's wife into the room. Death is an ugly thing: blood was spattered from the various times samples were taken and IV lines had been inserted. From the waist to the head, the body was deeply mottled in a purplish hue. The eyes were dilated and staring at the white ceiling tiles.

His wife had been hollering at the orderlies, "What is happening with my husband?"

Now she knew what had happened. At first, there were just sobs.

Then with a great wail of anguish, she cried out, "Wake up!"

Suddenly she began to beat on the chest of her deceased husband demanding, "Why did you leave me?"

I have thought of that day many times in the past thirty years. I suppose it is because of my surprise at her violent reaction to having lost her husband. What could have prepared his wife for his death?

It was as if a thief had broken in and stolen her prized possession and she had no chance to say, "Goodbye, dear."

Perhaps her husband might have had some warning signs, but did he act on them? Doctors can be unprepared, too, but they are the heroes in white coats (the good guys.) Could they have done something "heroic"? Did the deceased's doctor alert him to his condition? Did the patient listen? Death should not win, but in this case it did.

Then there is the preacher. If anyone should be alert, it is the pastor. I wonder if this man had an opportunity to trust Christ as his Savior? I wonder if a pastor ever visited him? Did a pastor ever warn him of a coming day when he would face his Creator? I recount this incident from my service days because it relates to the time in which we live currently. Churches in America have been asleep for a very long time. When one is asleep, one neither sees nor heeds God's warnings. The Lord of Glory warns His bride to be watchful.

When one is asleep, one neither sees nor heeds God's warnings. The Lord of Glory warns His bride to be watchful.

I have pastored churches in both the South and the North. I know people think those living in other areas of the country are different, but the truth is, not so much. Yes, the accent may be different, the food fried or not, but humanity is basically the same. Man is a rebellious creature and that is not a good thing according to God. If we search our hearts, we know they are not good. We do not like being told we have done something wrong. We do not like being awakened to our failings. This is true even of church people.

I have selected this passage of scripture from Revelation 3 because it graphically demonstrates a dead church that needs to be awakened. I am not going to try to equate a particular denomination with the church at Sardis. Rather, I want us to carefully study what Christ Jesus is saying here "to he that hath an ear." That would be me, as well as you, the reader.

Sardis, a Figure of Complacency

According to *The New Harper's Bible Dictionary*, 1973, Sardis was the capital of the Kingdom of Lydia around 1200 BC and an important trade crossing. Here is where the first coins were minted. Its inhabitants believed it to be unassailable.[1] In *History* by Herodotus, the following story of interest is recorded:

> "On the fourteenth day of siege Cyrus bade some horsemen ride about his lines, and make proclamation to the whole army that he would give a reward to the man who should first mount the wall. After this he made an assault,

1 The New Harper's Bible Dictionary. Madeleine S. and J. Lane Miller. New York. Harper and Row.1973, p. 645.

ree of them next to a puddle in our long dirt driveway:
rayfish. We have two ponds on our farm, and I guessed it h
ying to make its way from one to the other. Mark crouche
d the girls gathered around as he picked it up by its shell. I
d snapped its little claws in the air, beadily eyeballing us g
anaged, through force of will, to seem more formidable
e. I am 5'2" and married to a man who is 6'6", so I
ow how that feels.

The girls took turns holding it, passing
back and forth. They stuck twigs in
claws to test its strength, until I
minded them that dinner was on
e table. "Do you want to carry
to the pond?" Mark asked.
ne, the elder, squinted up at
im. "Dad?" she asked,
Could we eat it?" She had
ot yet developed a good
rasp of scale, and it
eminded her of the lobster
he'd savored at her grand-
other's house the summer
efore.

I made the noise, familiar
o my family, that expresses dis-
leasure without actually saying
o, and mentally collated my
oints of opposition. What was it
oing out of the water, anyway? Maybe
was sick. I knew from other culinary
ventures with my husband (hello, squirrel,
d you too, pigeon) that this project held poten-

but without success. His troops retired, but a certain Mardian, Hyroeades by name, resolved to approach the citadel and attempt it at a place where no guards were ever set...It is on that side of the city which faces Mount Tmolus. Hyroeades, however, having the day before observed a Lydian soldier descend the rock after a helmet rolled down from the top, and having seen him pick it up and carry it back, formed his plan. He climbed the rock himself, and other Persians followed in his track, until a large number had mounted to the top. Thus was Sardis taken..."[2]

In 214 B.C., the city fell to Antiochus the Great using the Persian method of more than three centuries earlier.

According to *Histories* by Polybius, "After these they selected thirty others, to remain in reserve at a certain distance; that, as soon as they had themselves climbed over the walls, and come to the nearest gate, the thirty might come up to it from the outside and try to knock

2 Herodotus, with an English translation by A. D. Godley. Cambridge. Harvard University Press. 1920, p. 84.

off the hinges and fastenings, while they on the inside cut the cross bar and bolt pins. They also selected two thousand men to follow behind the thirty, who were to rush into the town with them and seize the area of the theatre, which was a favourable position to hold against those on the citadel, as well as those in the town."[3]

So Sardis became a figure of complacency. Sleep is a kind of complacency, too. There are times that people believe themselves to be "too big to fail." We are living in such days. Just as the inhabitants of Sardis failed to learn that "their secret was out," churches can, if not careful, take on the attitudes and characteristics of their unsaved neighbors. I believe that the warning of Christ Jesus to Sardis, and to us, is especially valuable today.

Jesus began by saying that He knows their works. We who belong to God are watched by Him day and night. His is a loving watcher. It is always for our benefit. It is for our safety. But just as Sardis had an enemy looking for her vulnerability, so we also have an enemy who seeks a way in to destroy our testimony.

---

3 Histories. Polybius. Evelyn S. Shuckburgh. translator. London, New York. Macmillan. 1889. Reprint Bloomington 1962, p. 523.

Part of effectively using this armor is asking for His wisdom from above

Our Savior sees our works. He sees that we often fail to put on the full armor of God each day. He sees us leaning over the wall and losing our helmet. When going to retrieve it, we leave an open breach in the wall of our lives. You and I may think we have **all** the answers and do not need extra protection, but we are wrong. Only God's armor offers what we need. Part of effectively using this armor is asking for His wisdom from above. Do you and I seek Him out for His wisdom? He will not rebuke those who ask it of Him (James 1:5).

Jesus goes on to say that though this church has a reputation of being alive, He knows them to be dead. I think again of that lady years ago shouting to the lifeless body of her husband, "Wake up!" That which is dead cannot wake up. It is dead. There is no life.

We exude holiness when we give Him total control of our lives.

The word Jesus uses for life is often equated with holiness (2 Corinthians 5:4) and also with the gospel (2 Timothy 1:10). A church that is dead does not mean the people no longer have fellowship suppers. Nor does it mean that they are not as loving as they used to be. Those are symptoms of a serious problem, to be sure. No, dead means **dead**. A dead church is not a *holy* one. I do not mean the practiced, stylized, somber "holiness" of the Pharisees.

Jesus exuded true holiness because He was and is perfectly holy. We exude holiness when we give Him **total** control of our lives. The citizens of Sardis were not interested in keeping guard. They assumed nothing bad could ever happen to them. The members of the Sardis church likewise grew complacent. They **acted** holy. Their neighbors, and even some other Christians **thought** the fellowship at Sardis was holy, but that was not the case. Sardis also failed to share the gospel with the lost.

It has been my aim to be ready to share the good news that Christ has died for sinners with the lost as God gives me opportunity each day. It is also part of the good news that Jesus did not stay dead, but God raised Him up. This is the proof that He is the One and Only Savior of mankind! A person or a church body that does not **actively** seek to spread the gospel is dead. We are not talking about a "weak pulse" or "barely breathing." Jesus says dead.

What Is the Remedy?

Have you ever told your children, "Stop that hollering and racket! It is enough to wake the dead"? I am so glad that we have a Savior that **can** wake the **dead**. If you want to read about it, go to Matthew 9:24. A little girl had actually died, but to Jesus physical death was no more than a nap. If He has power over physical death, don't you think He can raise the spiritually dead as well? If the physically dead **hear** Him, can the unholy and play-acting church members do the same?

First, He orders the church to **wake up!** This means to **be watchful.** Scripture reminds us that watching for His return has a peculiar effect on Christians—watching make us holy. Having hope or a watchful expectation and longing for the return of the Master, has a purifying effect on us. So, **watch** for Him!

Beloved, now are we the sons of God, and it doth not yet appear what we shall be: but we know that, when he shall appear, we shall be like him; for we shall see him as he is. And every man that hath this hope in him purifieth himself, even as he is pure. (1 John 3:2-3)

Second, He commands they strengthen the remainder that is **about** to die. We ask the remainder of what? The remainder refers back to the deeds of which Jesus knew in verse one. They were **incomplete** deeds. An incomplete work is one that is on its way to the grave yard. It is interesting to see that our Lord views our works with very different eyes than we do. It really makes us think about standing before Him at the "bema" seat (2 Corinthians 5:10). In Roman courts, this seat was for the judge. We might also ask **who** was doing these weak, incomplete deeds, since the dead cannot do anything. Hopefully, by this time, the "sleeping dead zombies" had awakened.

Perhaps those who **are awake** are the ones He wants to use to strengthen the incomplete works. After all, we Christians need each other. We cannot do it alone. The gifts God gives each of us are for the building up of the church. We need to sound the alarm to sleeping brethren!

In verse five Jesus says there are a **few names** that have not defiled their garments. These are the garments of righteousness that every Christian has. We are clothed in the righteousness of Christ. When we act or behave in an unrighteous manner, we drag His precious Name through the mud. I hope tears have come to your eyes. A saint will weep when thinking of how we have failed our Lord. A spiritually dead person will have no feeling at all.

The "few names" are those who have not gone to sleep. They are the ones who, though not very strong spiritually, are still watching. They have not lost any armor over the wall. One thing is certain, the believer who is awake is his or her brother or sister's keeper. If you are awake, do you care enough to speak correction or even rebuke your yoke fellow? Those who do conduct their lives in purity for they are worthy. Worthy of what? They are worthy of the name by which they are called: Christian.

Finally, there is a warning from our Savior. If we fail to remember what we have received and what we have heard, we will not be waking up. We will remain dead. Jesus promises that He will come like a thief in the night (without warning) and it will be a total surprise which is not a good thing if we are still asleep. Have you decided that you or someone you know is asleep? Remind them or yourself of what **you** have received.

Jesus promises that He will come like a thief in the night (without warning) and it will be a total surprise which is not a good thing if we are still asleep.

You received the gift of eternal life through the shed blood of God's only begotten Son. You received this gift through hearing the gospel (Romans 10:13-15). Christ's warning is serious. A person that cannot be awakened is one that is spiritually dead. One may have **heard** the gospel and yet not have responded in faith. The spiritually dead have their names removed from the book of life. Eternal separation from God is the result.

Awake Action Steps

Before you move on to the next chapter, take a few minutes and do these Awake Action Steps.

> ➢ *"Repent,"* says Christ and become one who overcomes. This is a matter of agreeing with God we have been out of His will.
> ➢ Overwhelmed by sleep, one must seek restoration.
> ➢ Dead, one must seek to be raised.

These last two steps require asking Jesus to come into one's heart and be saved.

Heed the warning. Do not wait until it is too late!

CHAPTER 2

SLEEP AND READINESS

Then shall the kingdom of heaven be likened unto ten virgins, which took their lamps, and went forth to meet the bridegroom. And five of them were wise, and five were foolish. They that were foolish took their lamps, and took no oil with them: But the wise took oil in their vessels with their lamps. While the bridegroom tarried, they all slumbered and slept. And at midnight there was a cry made, Behold, the bridegroom cometh; go ye out to meet him. Then all those virgins arose, and trimmed their lamps. And the foolish said unto the wise, Give us of your oil; for our lamps are gone out. But the wise answered, saying, Not so; lest there be not enough for us and you: but go ye rather to them that sell, and buy for

yourselves. And while they went to buy, the bridegroom came; and they that were ready went in with him to the marriage: and the door was shut. Afterward came also the other virgins, saying, Lord, Lord, open to us. But he answered and said, Verily I say unto you, I know you not. Watch therefore, for ye know neither the day nor the hour wherein the Son of man cometh. (Matthew 25:1-13)

"*A* white-glove inspection," I murmured under my breath.

I was getting out of the Air Force. My family and I had been living in base quarters. The movers had come, packed everything, and left the day before. Now it was us and the cleaning supplies. The base had a policy that when a member "PCS'ed" (permanent change of station), their quarters were inspected, and had to be returned to the "perfectly clean" and original condition they had been in when you received the keys at the beginning of your duty. Of course, they wanted you to pay them the exorbitant sum of almost $600.00 to clean the quarters. That might not sound like much to you, but upon arrival in Florida, I would not have a job waiting for me. Every dime had to be accounted for, and this was just the beginning.

We stayed up all night washing every cabinet in the kitchen, inside and out. I used a toothbrush to clean out the tracks in the sliding windows. I used a high-pressure nozzle to wash the siding on the duplex. Oil stains had to come off the driveway. Fortunately, I did not have to remove the drywall and insulation I installed in the basement.

"We thought it had been done by us," was the comment the housing inspector made when determining whether to leave it or not.

We had been up for more than twenty-four hours when I had to get my family to the airport. We had sold our "daily driver" cars. I was going to drive to Florida in the old 1941 Ford I had restored as soon as our quarters passed inspection.

That afternoon, the housing official came and actually carried a white glove for the inspection.

When she finished, she said, "I have never seen quarters as clean as this. They are more spotless than when our team does the cleaning. If I had found anything wrong, you would still have had to pay for a cleaning, but as things are, you are free to leave."

As I drove down the road, I became incredibly sleepy. The old car had a working radio, but that did not help. It was almost August and the wool seats were scratchy, but **that** did not even help! It was then that I began to hear a drumming sound. After a few miles, I stopped and inspected the 500 X 16 wide-whitewall tires. Nothing wrong there. I had gotten about thirty miles south of the base when I noticed my ears were ringing. They kept on ringing even when the car was stopped and the quiet flat-head engine was off.

"I have got to get some sleep," I thought.

So I found a hotel at the next exit, and checked in. I did not eat first. I went to sleep. I slept from around 3:30 that afternoon until 9:00 AM the next morning. When you **have** to sleep, you sleep!

Parable of the Ten Virgins

The story Christ tells is about a wedding party who **had** to sleep. The parable of the ten virgins comes immediately after the close of Matthew 24 where Jesus answers His disciples questions regarding when the temple would be destroyed. They wanted to know how they could tell when His *parousia* or His appearing was about to happen. What would be the signs that would accompany the end of the age?

It is very important to keep the context of what we are reading in mind. When you take scripture out of context, you can make it say almost anything. That is not a good thing, and is very displeasing to God. The parable of the five wise and five foolish virgins follows immediately after this discussion on the end of the age.

There are several important issues to deal with in the setting of this story. First, Christ begins by labeling this a "Kingdom of heaven" story. This current life we live is preparation for our eternal home in God's Kingdom. As I related in my earlier book, *Life Is a Pop Quiz*, life is a series of tests or quizzes. Pop quizzes are "spot checks" to see if we are understanding the lessons.

The bridegroom in the story is very clearly Jesus Himself. The ten virgins or bridesmaids have been chosen to be in the wedding party. They represent those who say they are followers or believers in the bridegroom. All the maids are dressed appropriately. Clearly, they had been invited. All met the standards, but Jesus said that five were prudent and five were foolish or *morai* from which we get the word *moron*.

The deadly mistake they made is not being prepared.

In the first chapter of this book, I pointed out that the church at Sardis is upbraided for its "sleep of death." While sleep is often regarded as a failing, Jesus does not condemn the maidens for this. No, the deadly mistake they made is **not being prepared.** In the first century, the Jewish wedding was a big event that would last for days.

Of course we know from the story of Jesus' birth that Mary and Joseph were engaged, which was step one. The engagement was arranged by the fathers of the couple. Step two was the betrothal. This was a period of time for the groom to prepare a place for his bride and plan the wedding party. This could take up to a year. The final step would be the wedding feast, which could last for a week. The groom, often at night, would announce the beginning of the feast, and the attendants would form a parade to the site of the party. At the end of the feast, the groom and bride would be left alone to begin their life as "husband and wife." Each maiden knew what was expected of her.

I have an ancient oil lamp I purchased during my stay in Jerusalem some years ago. The small lamp is about 3 inches in diameter. Consequently, it can hold very little oil. If one was going to be out at night, and did not know how long the groom would be detained, a wise or prudent person would carry extra oil for the parade.

It is interesting to me that Jesus sets the time of the groom's *parousia* at midnight. Midnight is often thought of as the "darkest hour." It is surely the time that will find most sleeping. Today, the church finds herself in a very dark hour. It seems that leaders of governments believe that the world and its nations are in a "post-Christian" time. They think they do not have to listen to or heed these Christian people. The warnings of their ancient Bible no longer have any meaning for them. It is a very dark time indeed.

The prophet Daniel says, "And he (the lawless one) shall speak great words against the most High, and shall wear out the saints of the most High, and think to change times and laws: and they shall be given into his hand until a time and times and the dividing of time" (Daniel 7:25).

I do not know about you, but there are many times that I feel tired. I tire of seeing and hearing all the evil that gushes forth from every conceivable source. I tire of trying to wake up sleeping saints.

It is no wonder that some church members say, "Do not bother, just let them sleep."

It is also no wonder that others begin to doze off and sleep. The trouble is, when you see sleeping church members, how do you tell the real apart from the counterfeit?

The church has largely settled for simulating holiness and the working of the Holy Spirit instead of submitting to Him.

One way is by "checking the oil." In old cars, like the '41 Ford I spoke of earlier, you really did need to check the oil every so many hours or miles. Oil is the life blood of an engine. Run low on oil and gas consumption increases. Run out of oil, and the engine is dead—it grinds to a stop.

There have been so many different concepts of how Christians are to obtain "the oil of holiness." Some became involved in pietism. In the late 15th century, an awareness was building in western Christianity that something was wrong in the faith. Pietism was one response that tried emphasizing certain lost doctrines of the apostles. Most ended up emphasizing preaching, prayer, evangelism or other early church characteristics.

In the late 19th century, feelings and emotion became the way to tell if you were "filled with the Spirit." Today, churches are engaged in "warring" over worship styles and different types of music for much the same reason. I have found that man-made denominations result from believers who are either genuinely concerned about something wrong in their church or are just disgruntled with the *status quo*.

Instead of turning to God in repentance, they either over- or under-emphasize a particular apostolic teaching. Cults, on the other hand, oppose and contradict the apostles' teaching. In any case, the church has largely **settled** for **simulating** holiness and the working of the Holy Spirit instead of **submitting** to Him. For the Christian, oil represents the Holy Spirit. Having oil represents readiness. It is being owned by and filled with the Spirit. Nighttime can make waiting seem awfully long. The point Jesus is making is that the appointed time for His Glorious Appearing is unknown to us and the angels.

Waking the Foolish Virgins

Bright light in the eyes of the sleeping can hurt. It can result in our giving a cross response. See what happens when the foolish virgins awake and realize their dilemma.

First, they try to buy some oil from the wise virgins. The wise virgins **cannot** sell their oil.

I am reminded of Simon the magician, who was said to have become a believer (Acts 8:9-23.) When he saw that the Holy Spirit came to believers as the apostles laid their hands on them, he wanted to "buy this power." He literally wanted to buy the Holy Spirit from the apostles, much as the foolish virgins wanted to purchase oil. For this he received a scathing rebuke from Peter, "Thy money perish with thee, because thou hast thought that the gift of God may be purchased with money" (Acts 8:20). Simon may have **believed**, but it was not a **saving** belief.

Second, as the foolish maidens go to buy more oil, the wise participate in the parade that leads to the feast, and then the door is shut. When the foolish find the party, they plead, "Let us in!" This time it is the Bridegroom who appears at the door saying, "Truly, I say to you, I do not know you." He was really saying to them, "You may have said you were chosen to go to the party, but your carelessness, and lack of concern says otherwise. If you had really wanted to participate, you would have been ready." No one wants to hear the Lord of Glory say, "I do not know you."

There is one other wedding story Jesus tells. I am inserting it here as it has given me some food for thought lately. In Matthew 22:1-14, Jesus is responding to His rejection by the religious authorities. He tells of a king who is preparing a feast for his son's wedding. Many are invited to come, but these potential guests turn their noses up at the invitation, and some even seize and kill the king's servants. It is easy to understand that Christ is referring to the rejection of both the gospel and God's servants. After the king executes revenge, like the destruction of Jerusalem in 70 A.D., he invites others because the original guests "were not worthy."

Here is the curious part of that story that we also need to ponder. The king finds one person not dressed in wedding clothes. The king asks him how he got into the party without the appropriate clothing. Garments of righteousness are the wedding clothes for those at the marriage of the Lamb (Revelation 19:8.) The intruder is speechless. The servants are told to bind this uninvited guest "hand and foot" and toss him into the outer darkness. We are told the place to which he is sent is a place of "weeping and gnashing of teeth. For many are called but few are chosen."

I have long considered what the heavenly wedding feast of the bride of Christ will be like (Revelation 19:5-10.) We know that at the conclusion of the feast, Jesus sets out on His white horse to end the battle outside Jerusalem accompanied by the host of heaven. We are there with Him. We also know that, prior to this, Satan and his fellow fallen angels have been thrown out of heaven as "neither was their place found any more in heaven" (Revelation 12:8).

Can you imagine having a wedding feast, and suddenly Satan shows up? It would be like having a repo-man trying to get the tables and glassware from the banquet hall. Unthinkable! Yet we know that the enemy has had access to God's throne since the time he rebelled (Job 1:6). It seems likely to me that at the same time that God takes His church up for the feast, the enemy and his hoard are thrown down. I have wondered if the one who is found without the wedding garment (righteous clothing) could be one of the old dragon's angels who had been "hiding" in heaven?

There is one thing that is certain. Only those whom God has proclaimed righteous can be admitted to the feast. This clearly leaves atheists outside in the "gnashing of teeth" area. It also clearly illustrates that the casual "Christian" does not know the Lord, and the Lord certainly does not know him or her.

Awake Action Steps

Before you move on to the next chapter, take a few minutes and do these Awake Action Steps.

> ➤ The deadly mistake the ten virgins made was **not being prepared.** Search your heart and ask yourself:

Am I aware of this hour of darkness?
Am I prepared to stand before the Bridegroom
and give an account of all the works
I have done in the flesh?
Are my works done in the strength and power
of His Holy Spirit?
Are they resulting from selfish deeds?
Am I spiritually ready should Christ tarry in
His coming back for me?
Am I really prepared?
Am I play-acting or earnestly seeking
His guidance and doing His will?

CHAPTER 3

SPIRITUAL SLEEP

Love not sleep, lest thou come to poverty; open thine eyes, and thou shalt be satisfied with bread. (Proverbs 20:13)

How long wilt thou sleep, O sluggard? When wilt thou arise out of thy sleep? Yet a little sleep, a little slumber, a little folding of the hands to sleep: So shall thy poverty come as one that travelleth, and thy want as an armed man. (Proverbs 6:9-11)

There is a considerable similarity between physical sleep and the kind that God's Word warns against. In Proverbs there are many different topics that deal with life and how one conducts oneself such as integrity, truthfulness, knowledge, keeping a vow, loyalty, honor, and the ways of the Lord are positive. As is often the case when giving advice, there are far more warnings against bad behavior than encouragements of good conduct. Why would this be?

Jeremiah 17:9 answers saying, "The heart is deceitful above all things, and desperately wicked: who can know it?" This is why in Proverbs 20:13 God finds it needful to warn us about intoxication, anger, laziness, defrauding, gossip, lying, slandering, cursing one's parents, rash words, and **loving sleep**. What an interesting mix! No one can say that God is not interested in character development. By placing these serious character flaws in a common group, God is not encouraging us to try to develop a system of "which sin is worse." Rather, He is saying that all such sins are deplorable and an abomination in His sight.

In fact, He uses the word abomination in verses ten and twenty-three in regard to defrauding others. The Hebrew word *to-ay-baw'* (abomination) gives the sense that it is a disgusting practice. That is the problem we have with sin. We practice it. We deceive ourselves by doing so. The more it is part of one's life-style, the more "natural" it seems. This is true because man's nature is sinful and fallen. Man was not created this way, but because of Adam's choice we are born this way. No wonder we need a Savior!

Friendship with Sleep

Getting back to the topic of sleep, please notice that it is not sleep that is wicked. The apostle Paul reminded Timothy, " For the **love** of money is the root of all evil: which while some coveted after, they have erred from the faith, and pierced themselves through with many sorrows" (1 Timothy 6:10). In the same manner it is the **love** of sleep where poverty begins. It is interesting how God pairs the sources of greed and poverty together! Both produce sorrow and pain. They both come from having an **affection/ love toward (aw-hab') or friendship with (phil-a)** a thing: sleep in the former case, and money in the latter.

If Christians are to awake from sleep, their desire must be for the One Who is the "Bread of Life."

When God instructs us to open our eyes, it is more than just a literal "wake-up call." Spiritually we must realize that the desire of the sleeping heart is for something that impoverishes us—loss of consciousness toward God. This kind of sleep ignores Bible study and meditation. It forgets about prayer. It does not have a Christo-centric world view.

If Christians are to awake from sleep, their desire must be for the One Who is the "Bread of Life."

The One Who was born in "The House of Bread" (Bethlehem) is our satisfaction. When we awaken from our lethargy and let the Spirit have His way with us, then we will know His strength and riches. We shall no longer be spiritually impoverished. How did this "sleeping sickness" sneak up on us?

Have you ever said, "I am so tired of this or that?"

We **do** get tired. In fact, Daniel says that in the end of days "And he (man of sin) shall speak great words against the most High, and shall **wear out the saints of the most High**, and think to change times and laws: and they shall be given into his hand until a time and times and the dividing of time" (7:25 emphasis added). Well, we are fast approaching that time.

The problem is, we did not start down the road of sleep intentionally. No, we first thought, "I'll just take a little nap. No big deal. After all, I need my 'beauty sleep'." The difference between sleep (*shay-naw'*) and slumber (*ten-oo-maw'*) is that slumber refers to drowsiness. Drowsiness begins by "folding the hands."

When you and I decide to put down the written sword of the Lord, we are stopping the "good fight" Paul referred to (2 Timothy 4:7) and are preparing to get slothful (*aw-tsale'*). Proverbs 6:9 refers to the sluggard or indolent, lazy person who forgets that Jesus Christ commissioned them to spread the gospel and make disciples. They cannot be bothered about Paul's "good fight." In fact, the person who worries incessantly about "confrontation" with the world, the flesh, and the devil is not just asleep, that individual is **comatose**!

Is the church in this danger today? Next Sunday or Wednesday, open your spiritual eyes and let God help you see your church. What percentage of your membership attends? Do you have discipleship classes, such as Sunday School? What percentage attends prayer meeting? Now do not be one of those who say, "Nickels and noses that is all you care about." The early church counted noses (and shekels). Just read the book of Acts or any of Paul's letters where he asked for offerings. Those who don't *want* to count, really don't *count* **where** it counts.

Samson

The clearest illustration in the Bible of what spiritual sleep of the saint actually looks like can be found in Judges 13 through 16. It is the story of Samson. Samson belongs in the list of saints. Why? **First,** we have his conception announced by a heavenly messenger. His father, Manoah (meaning rest or quiet), is from the tribe of Dan (meaning a judge), living in the town of Zorah (or scourge). The messenger appears to

Manoah's barren wife and tells her she will have a son who is to be raised according to the Nazirite tradition. Upon hearing his wife's account, Manoah asks God to send the messenger back to both of them for further instruction. The messenger returns to his wife, who is in a field. She runs to find her husband and bring him to the messenger. **Second,** this brings us to the identity of "the Angel of the Lord." When asked if he is the same "man," the angel replies with "I am," or *haw-yaw'* which is I exist. This reply was used by Christ in John 18:5 when He was being arrested. The Greek word *i-mee'* also means I exist. The reason the arresting crowd fell down upon hearing His declaration of identity was due to Christ answering them as "I Am" or Jehovah.

Manoah invites the angel to stay for a meal, which the angel declines. Instead he urges Manoah to prepare a burnt offering unto the Lord. Then he asks "the man" his name so that they may honor him. The angel says, "Why seekest thou thus after my name, seeing it is *wonderful (paw-lee')*?" *Paw-lee'* means secret or wonderful and is one of the names for the Messiah in Isaiah 9:6, *peh'-leh*. Both come from the word *paw-law'* which means to accomplish difficult, high or wonderful things.

41

Did Manoah think this was "good news" for them? You be the judge: "The angel of the Lord ascended in the flame of the altar. And Manoah and his wife looked on it, and fell on their faces to the ground.... And Manoah said unto his wife, We shall surely die, because we have seen God" (Judges 13:20, 22).

Third, we have the testimony of the Bible itself. In Hebrews 11:32 we have Samson's name listed in the company of those who conquered by faith. Since we have God intervening to bring about his birth, a theophany of the pre-incarnate Christ, and the statement in Hebrews, one must conclude the life of Samson to be an example to us. Samson's role as judge and his required devotion to God as a Nazirite were effective against God's enemies.

However, Samson's failure to live up to all the obligations of a Nazirite limited that effectiveness. As one looks at Samson's life, we see a series of "sleepwalking" snapshots. There was to be no eating or drinking of any grape product, no wine or strong drink, no eating of any meat that is unclean, and no cutting of his hair. Yet Samson did not heed all of the divine instructions. His first encounter with a Philistine woman had been ordained of the Lord (Judges 14:4), but women who did not fear the Lord proved to be his downfall. Jewish women held no appeal for the judge of Israel.

The Philistines learned that a woman's tears could make Samson reveal his secrets (verse 17). In all these matters, Samson seems to have categorized God's commands into those he must obey and those he can skip. As Samson progresses through life, his focus becomes more on things that please him and less on pleasing the Lord. While the Philistines were kept from attacking Israel by this "super judge," Samson's testimony in later life did not honor God the way it did earlier in his walk with the Lord.

His wandering eye having overpowered him, he fell to the clever Delilah. It is most interesting that his final act of disobedience resulted from **sleepwalking away from** God. Samson told her his secret, and while he slept she cut his hair.

And he awoke out of his sleep, and said, I will go out as at other times before, and shake myself. And he wist not that the Lord was departed from him. (Judges 16:20)

There comes a time when judgment must be made. Tragically, those who snooze actually do lose. We have one distinct advantage over Samson. Christ told us, "and, lo, I am with you alway, even unto the end of the age" (Matthew 28:20). This is why I believe that the **true** church **will** wake up. He will not allow those who have been born again to remain asleep. Those who **are born again** have the Holy Spirit dwelling within them. He is our alarm clock.

Awake Action Steps

Before you move on to the next chapter, take a few minutes and do these Awake Action Steps.

➢ Read the scriptures from Proverbs concerning slothfulness and laziness. Record what the Holy Spirit reveals to you from these scriptures.

Proverbs 6:9-11

Proverbs 20:13

➢ Read the story of Samson in Judges 13-16. What lessons did you learn from his story that you can apply to your own life?

➢ What promise did Jesus make to you in Matthew 28:20?

CHAPTER 4

THE IMPORTANCE OF LIGHT

And that, knowing the time, that now it is high time to awake out of sleep: for now is our salvation nearer than when we believed. The night is far spent, the day is at hand: let us therefore cast off the works of darkness, and let us put on the armour of light. (Romans 13:11-12)

But all things that are reproved are made manifest by the light: for whatsoever doth make manifest is light. Wherefore he saith, Awake thou that sleepest, and arise from the dead, and Christ shall give thee light. (Ephesians 5:13-14)

*S*hortly after the events of 9-11, I took a trip to Israel. It was a moving experience. On the flight over, I had a planned layover in London. When

45

I was on the plane to England, there were very few people traveling due to the recent events in the U. S. I had practically an entire 747 to myself. Actually, I think there were more crew members than passengers. As a result, I was able to lie down across a row of seats and sleep in the darkened cabin. While in London, I had the opportunity to see Trafalgar Square, watch the changing of the guard at Buckingham Palace, see Number 10 Downing Street, and other sights. The significance for me is that I was walking in the same place that previous generations of Scrimshaws walked and lived. After a day in England, I took an *El Al* flight to Tel Aviv, and arrived in the blessed land around 4 AM.

The taxi ride to Jerusalem, where I lodged at the YMCA across the street from the King David Hotel, was really interesting. I shared a taxi with an Eastern Orthodox priest, an Orthodox rabbi, a Roman Catholic priest, and a businessman. I know it sounds like the beginning of a joke, but it is the simple truth.

One of the things I remember was hearing the birds sing their "good morning" songs. Israel is under the flight path of countless European, Asian, and African birds—simply amazing! It is no wonder that Solomon had such an inquisitive mind with all the varieties of life to examine. By the time I arrived at my hotel, the sun was well up in the sky and I was suffering from the disruption of my circadian rhythm. The length of exposure to light is not the problem, but the experience of daylight and darkness which is opposite to what the body is accustomed becomes the issue.

It is normally difficult to sleep when there is much light flooding one's room, but "jet lag" has a way of making you find rest despite the early-rising sunlight that somehow penetrates the eyelids. I imagine the modern Jebusites are accustomed to their time zone. It would be easy for me to begin telling you more about Israel, but the reason I am recounting this particular story is because of the effect of light on sleep.

The issue of light also arises in the spiritual realm for the Christian. It is easy to sleep in a spiritual sense when we maintain a darkened lifestyle. I believe that is what the Apostle Paul is getting at in the text at the beginning of this chapter. Paul begins with the statement that we know the time. The Greek word he uses for time is *kairos*, meaning an age or era. The Bible recognizes periods or eras in which God has specific purposes for His redemptive plan. The difficulty is for Christians to recognize the era that they occupy.

In 1 Chronicles 12:32, we read that men from the tribe of Issachar had an understanding of the times in which they lived and combined it with knowledge of what their people should do. It is this kind of wisdom that is so desperately needed in the church today. So many churches have either wrongly taught the Word of God or forsaken the Great Commission of Matthew 28, which instructs us to make disciples. Members of these churches have little concern for the spiritual things of God. It can be said that many believers are as blind to spiritual truth as their unbelieving neighbors.

It is easy to sleep in a spiritual sense when we maintain a darkened lifestyle.

Today there are many who simply do not believe in the return of Christ. Some scoffers note that Paul cried out to Christians of his day with an obvious urgency in regard to the return of Christ. Yet here we are still waiting almost 2000 years later for Christ's return. This is why Peter warned the following:

Knowing this first, that there shall come in the last days scoffers, walking after their own lusts, and saying, Where is the promise of his coming? For since the fathers fell asleep, all things continue as they were from the beginning of the creation." (2 Peter 3:3-4)

There are also those who wonder at Paul's expectancy of the "Blessed Hope." It is important to remember that for Paul, Israel occupied the land, the temple was still standing, the daily sacrifices were still ongoing, and the abomination mentioned in Daniel 9:27 might occur at any moment. All the prophetic elements were in existence for Christ to make His appearance. It was up to the church to spread the gospel to the ends of the earth. In Romans 10:18 Paul said, "But I say, Have they not heard? Yes, verily, their sound went into all the earth, and their words unto the ends of the world." It was certainly not a time to be asleep. Yet some in the church were asleep even at its beginning. Paul seems to be almost shouting at the Romans when he tells them it is already the hour that we should be roused out of sleep. What does he mean?

First, Paul mentions that our salvation is nearer than when we believed. Many become confused by this. They think that the day they believed was "the day of their salvation." In part, this is true. There was a day when we first believed. It is, in effect, our spiritual birthday. However, sanctification is a process in which God fashions us into the likeness of His Son. This process of sanctification culminates in our own resurrection. If you are not undergoing "a holy change," then you have believed with your mind on an intellectual level, but not with your heart on a spiritual level. The day of our ultimate salvation is when we shall see Christ and be like Him. Those who have died believing in Jesus as their Lord and Savior know a rest that is beyond understanding. The fullest expression of salvation awaits them when they receive their resurrection body.

Second, he states that the night is advanced. There are some preachers and theologians who teach that we can find God in darkness. Yet Scripture reveals that God is our Heavenly "Father of lights, with whom is no variableness, neither shadow of turning" (James 1:17). We can avoid neither the literal night of earth, nor the spiritual night of mankind's sin. It is all around us. It is also part of man's nature. Know this, however, that as night advances toward its final unraveling, the day is about to break forth which Paul speaks is the light of truth. This truth is not a fact but a person—Christ Jesus. He is coming back and His *parousia* or appearing will be sudden and without warning.

Third, Paul says that the day is drawing nigh. He recognizes that the stars are disappearing from the sky. When I was a high school teacher in Florida, my first order of business upon arrival would be to station myself at a particular location at a covered porch and monitor the students as they arrived. During certain times of the year, after daylight savings time was over, the sky would be dark then. I noticed that as the hour progressed, the stars would begin disappearing. In one respect, the sky becomes darkest just before it begins to glow in the east. Friend, that is the time we find ourselves in. Man's wicked plans, as they are discovered, have never been darker. **Now** is **not** the time to sleep! The light of the world is about to dawn!

I believe that the growing darkness of this hour has made some pull the covers up over their heads to keep out the light. They want to sleep. This is the response Paul addressed in Ephesians 5:13-14. He said that some believers were asleep and needed to be awakened from the dead. I remember a preacher from the past who said that he knew that his church folks were going up in the resurrection first. When asked how he could possibly know this, he quoted the Scripture that said, "The dead in Christ shall rise first..."

Sleep is defined in Webster's Ninth New Collegiate Dictionary as "the natural periodic suspension of consciousness ..." (or) "to be in a state (as of quiescence or death) resembling sleep." When the believer becomes so lazy and complacent as to appear to be spiritually dead, then it is certainly "high time" to sound the alarm! That church member who is willfully not conscious and is unresponsive to the things of God is indeed in danger.

Put on the Armor of Light

Have you ever noticed that upon getting up from a nap or from a long sleep that you feel cold? Many of us rush over to the thermostat and raise it up in the morning for this very reason. Paul says we should lay aside the deeds of darkness. The sins that have acted as blankets to keep us asleep must be cast off! When sleeping Christians stir themselves from spiritual sleep, they should put on the armor of light.

> *But ye, brethren, are not in darkness, that that day should overtake you as a thief. Ye are all the children of light, and the children of the day: we are not of the night, nor of darkness. Therefore let us not sleep, as do others; but let us **watch** and **be sober**. For they that sleep, sleep in the night; and they that be drunken are drunken in the night. But let us, who are of the day, be sober, putting on the breastplate of faith and love; and for an helmet, the hope of salvation. For God hath not appointed us to wrath, but to obtain salvation by our Lord Jesus Christ, Who died for us, that, whether we wake*

or sleep (die), *we should live together with him.*
(1 Thessalonians 5:4-10 emphasis added)

The armor of light is clearly the full armor of God found in Ephesians 6:10-18. Without light, all plant life would die. Without light, and its accompanying warmth, the earth would freeze solid. May the Light of the world beam into the sleeping believer's heart and warm it! May the light of the Word rouse the sleeping Christian and make him live for Christ today!

Awake Action Steps

Before you move on to the next chapter, take a few minutes and do these Awake Action Steps.

> ➢ Read 1 Chronicles 12:32. What was so unique about the men from the tribe of Issachar?
> ➢ Define sanctification:
> ➢ Truth is not a fact but a person: _____
> ➢ The armor of light is defined in Ephesians 6:10-18. What is it?

Are you concerned about what the Lord is doing in creation?
Are you concerned about His return and how He will find you?
Then wake up!

CHAPTER 5

WHAT DO WE DO?

Therefore be ye also ready: for in such an hour as ye think not the Son of man cometh. (Matthew 24:44)

Beloved, now are we the sons of God, and it doth not yet appear what we shall be: but we know that, when he shall appear, we shall be like him; for we shall see him as he is. And every man that hath this hope in him purifieth himself, even as he is pure. (1 John 3:2-3)

And said unto them, Why sleep ye? rise and pray, lest ye enter into temptation. And while he yet spake, behold a multitude, and he that was called Judas, one of the twelve, went before them, and drew near unto Jesus to kiss

him. But Jesus said unto him, Judas, betrayest
thou the Son of man with a kiss? When they
which were about him saw what would follow,
they said unto him, Lord, shall we smite with
the sword? And one of them smote the servant
of the high priest, and cut off his right ear.
And Jesus answered and said, Suffer ye thus
far. And he touched his ear, and healed him.
(Luke 22:46-51)

There is a story reported about Charles Spurgeon regarding his thoughts on the return of Christ. Once, when asked if he thought Christ might return soon, he said, "I think not!"

After repeating this answer several times, someone finally became bold enough to ask him, "Doesn't the Bible demand that we anticipate Christ's coming? Why do you say, 'I think not!'?"

Spurgeon answered, "Because the Bible says, 'in such an hour as ye think not, the Son of Man cometh'."

Why is it, that when we read the life stories of the great heroes of our faith, there seems to be a prominent anticipation of seeing the Lord's return to earth? Could it be that such an expectation has something to do with the way they lived out their lives? You may have noticed that as we have looked into what the

Word of God has to say about watchfulness and spiritual sleep, there is a connection to prayer, temptation, and purity. With a basic understanding of these topics, let us look more deeply into the significance of these warning words of the Lord.   We have looked at the temptation to sleep in detail. What is Jesus warning us against in Matthew 24:44? Beginning in verse 36, Jesus had been warning of the sudden destruction that is coming for the disobedient. Then in verse 42 He warns believers, "**Ye** know not what hour **your** Lord doth come." Christ is not Lord to the lost, but He **is our** Lord. So what is this hour He refers to?

Watch

In Romans 13:11 Paul spoke of the hour or "high time." He was saying that a specific time had arrived and it was later than most of us would have thought it to be. Jesus is referring to a specific time for an appointed action—His return for His bride. Thus He instructs us **to watch**. The word translated **watch** is also the Greek root for a person's name: Gregory. One who is watchful or a watcher is spiritually alert, staying awake or vigilant. Such a person exhibits a certain amount of self-discipline. One must maintain an edge, as it were, to "be sharp." This is implied in the old saying, "Don't let the grass grow under your feet."

So what should we be watching for? The example Jesus gives is of a thief breaking into a house. My brother was a detective in the Miami Beach police department. He noted that burglaries usually had a certain amount of planning by the burglar. Hence there are things people should be aware of concerning their property. Have you ever been going about your daily routine and noticed that someone you had never seen before was watching you? He was noting your arrival and departure from a certain location and time. He was "casing you."

It has been said that most people go through life never looking up. They have their head **down**, **watching** the path they trod, unaware of what is going on around them. It is a kind of sleep-walking without being technically asleep. Now the burglar is not going to tell you when he plans to break into your home. Your only defense is to be vigilant (watchful).

What are the signs of Jesus' return? Do you see them? When studying the history of the times of Christ's first advent, there was a general anticipation of something great about to happen among the nations of the world. You can read of these expectations in the writings of Roman and Greek writers, as well as those of other nations of that day. It is interesting that something of a similar magnitude of expectation is being heard and felt around the world today. With such an awareness on the part of so many, though certainly not all people of the world, one can say there is a degree of "vigilance" on the part of a great number of people.

Be Ready

This leads us to Christ's injunction for us to "be ready." Being ready is to be prepared. Have you ever wondered what "prepared mustard" is? It is not mustard that is ready to jump on your hotdog. It means that someone has taken the time to combine dry mustard with the right type of seasonings and spices to make a specially-flavored condiment.

When a boy scout says that scouts need to "be prepared," they mean they are ready for whatever exigency that may occur. If there is an injury, they must know how to provide first aid. An emergency is coming rapidly to this world, the likes of which have never been seen before (Matthew 24:21).

Do you know what to do?
Can you give someone spiritual first aid?

Our mission, as believers in Christ Jesus, is to tell those who do not know Jesus as their Savior how they can **come** to know Him. You cannot do this in your sleep.

Confess

You may be thinking, "But I have not been a very good Christian. I have not put Him first in my life." Or you may say, "I have not lived a holy life–I have committed many of the sins listed by Paul in Romans 13:13: rioting and drunkenness, chambering and wantonness, strife and envying." Have you confessed these to God?

Confession means more than admitting to committing certain acts. Confession means agreeing with God that such things are wrong **and** that you no longer want to do them. Have you asked for God's forgiveness?

> *If we confess our sins, he is faithful and just to forgive us our sins, and to cleanse us from all unrighteousness.* (1 John 1:9)

Hope

What can purify us? There is a hope in Christ's manifestation that acts as a cleansing agent when applied to our hearts and minds (1 John 3:3). This word is used in Matthew 24:30 regarding the **manifestation** of the sign of the Son of Man, "immediately after the tribulation of those days." We have hope as believers that none other have. It is not a "hope so" kind of hope. It is a faith or "trust in" kind of hope.

The thought, which should ever be in the front of our minds is, "Today, I could meet Jesus. Would He find me serving Him and others? What would He find me doing?" These are thoughts that act as a purging and purifying cleanser. These only have that effect on people who understand the cost to God's only begotten Son on the cross of Calvary. Only those who have been regenerated or born again can appreciate the price He paid.

This thought reminds me of the "frontlets between thine eyes" that Israelites were commanded to bind on their heads in Deuteronomy 6:8. These leather boxes contained the *shema*.

Hear, O Israel: The LORD our God is one LORD: And thou shalt love the LORD thy God with all thine heart, and with all thy soul, and with all thy might." (Deuteronomy 6:4-5)

For the believer in Christ, we have the blessed hope written without hands on our minds and hearts.

What happens when Christians are not prepared?
What happens if they are caught snoozing and
must awake suddenly?
How is one tempted to act?

I believe that this can be seen in the actions of the disciples who were with Christ in Gethsemane. Earlier Jesus had told His disciples that the Shepherd was going to be struck, referring to His arrest and crucifixion. The sheep, His disciples, would be scattered. Bold Peter testified that even if the others forsook Jesus, he never would. It is here that we are afforded a glimpse into the heavenlies. Jesus tells Peter that Satan desired to "sift him like wheat," but He is praying for Peter's restoration so that he would be able to strengthen his fellow apostles. Later, in the Garden of Gethsemane, Jesus again instructs the disciples to "watch and pray," but none did. When the moment of betrayal occurred, they were unprepared.

Let us review His instructions for them. Did any stay awake? No, not one. Did any seek God's help in prayer? No, that is pretty hard to do in your sleep. When you have just awakened from a nap and find yourself surrounded by cops, what do you do?

Notice Luke 22:49. They had not remained alert or vigilant so they were not ready to follow any direction from God. In fact, they had not even prayed to God to find out what they should be doing! Peter did not even wait for Jesus to answer the question voiced by the disciples about defending themselves. Peter literally lashed out at the nearest head, Malchus, servant to the High Priest (John 18:10.)

Resist Temptation

At Caesarea Philippi, Peter had told Jesus that He would not die, thus earning Jesus' rebuke, "Get thee behind Me, Satan." Now we see similar behavior from Peter's hand that would thwart God's plan of salvation. How do I know? It is because Jesus says, "Put up thy sword into the sheath: the cup which my Father hath given me, shall I not drink it?"

When we are not alert and not "prayed-up," we become a tool for the enemy. Luke 22:51 adds Jesus' words, "Enough of this." Then He healed the man's ear. Think of it! The last healing Jesus would perform before his death was a result of Peter's impulsiveness. Having neither remained awake nor having prayed, Peter was in no position to resist the temptation of his temperament.

The command in the garden was to watch, pray, and resist temptation. The command to the end-time believer is the same. The results of ignoring our

Lord's commands are shame and sorrow. Do not be unprepared. Pray up! Stay up! Be ready to go up!

Awake Action Steps

Before you move on to the next chapter, take a few minutes and do these Awake Action Steps.

➢ Define a watcher:

Are you a watcher?

➢ Define vigilant:

Are you vigilant?

➢ What does it mean to be prepared for Christ's return?

Are you prepared?

Can you give someone spiritual first aid?

➢ Define confession:

Have you confessed your sins to God and asked Him for forgiveness?

➢ What is the hope believers have that none other have?

Do you have that hope?

➢ What happens when Christians are not prepared?

➢ When we are not alert and not "prayed-up," we become a tool for the _____.

➢ The command in the garden was to _____,

_____, and _____

_____.

CHAPTER 6

DO NOT BE DECEIVED

*Then if any man shall say unto you, Lo, here is Christ, or there; believe it not. For there shall arise false Christs, and false prophets, and shall shew great signs and wonders; insomuch that, **if** it were **possible**, they shall deceive the very elect. Behold, I have told you before. Wherefore if they shall say unto you, Behold, he is in the desert; **go not forth**: behold, he is in the secret chambers; believe it not. For as the lightning cometh out of the east, and shineth even unto the west; so shall also the coming of the Son of man be. For wheresoever the carcase is, there will the eagles be gathered together.* (Matthew 24:23-28 emphasis added)

*A*s a new chaplain, there was a great deal to learn. One of the responsibilities I had was called "ministry of presence." In the early 1980s at the base where I conducted my reserve training and duty, I was given my assignments of organizations and squadrons where I would visit with the Airmen and others attached to those units. The purpose was for my familiarization with the men and their mission in order to support them in spiritual needs they might have. I visited fire-fighters, fighter pilots, jet engine mechanics, and supply units. I also was assigned the "FTD." When I saw this designation, I jokingly asked my supervisor whether the Air Force was in the business of sending flowers. I soon learned that these letters stood for "Foreign Technologies Division."

When I arrived at the building with the FTD sign in front of it, I met one of the men attached to the unit. The building had no windows. Once inside the lobby, I saw that the door leading to the rest of the building was electrically locked. The individual who was my contact said that since I did not have a high level of security clearance, I would have to remain in the lobby. Naively, I asked what they did.

He said, "Well, about the only thing I can tell you is that we monitor technological development in other countries."

When I asked how this could be done, he replied, "Did you notice that there are no windows in this building? That is because satellites can be positioned on the horizon to look directly into a window."

He went on to tell me the kind of "spy games" that are played between nations. He told me the following story, which was several years old and now declassified. It seems they had been watching a particular ship yard in the former Soviet Union and decided to play a "head game" with one of the Russian workers. They sent a message to the man, congratulating him on his efforts to quit smoking. They had been daily counting the number of cigarettes in the package he carried in his shirt pocket. This had gone on for several weeks, enabling them to determine that he was smoking fewer of the cancer sticks.

"Of course, we have much better satellite resolution now. We can count the dimples on a golf ball as it lays on the green," he added.

When I asked if our adversaries had similar capabilities, he replied, "Sure, they do the same thing with us."

Then I asked a question, the answer to which has been in my mind ever since, "What is the purpose of making things top secret, if both sides know what the other is doing?"

"The purpose of government secrets is not so much keeping things from other governments as it is **keeping secrets from our own people**," he said.

I have told this story because it helps Christians to understand **why** they need to be awake. If the country that is supposedly your "enemy" is someone you are not afraid of, then what does it mean when you concentrate on keeping secrets from your fellow countrymen? Are you afraid of them? What sort of "foreign technology" do you **not** want them to know? Whom are you trying to "fool"?

Magical Thinking

Before I place the pieces of the puzzle out for you, I want to explain something called "magical thinking." This was one of the subjects I dealt with when teaching Sociology many years ago. Magical thinking is something humans often do, even in "technologically advanced" nations. Simply put, it is thinking that objects that resemble each other are somehow connected to each other in a real way. The objects can be real or touchable. They can be events in a dream or they can also be observable, as in sounds or something that can be seen. The key to understanding magical thinking is the linking together of these two things in a causal manner or saying, "this sight is caused by this person."

A magician will tell you that what he wants to do is to fool you, the observer. This is much how our Enemy, Satan, operates. How does a magician do this? He starts with what he knows you believe or do not believe. His aim is to have you suspend belief, which means successfully fool you. He does this by connecting two visual events that contradict your beliefs but are undeniable.

Do you recall the famous magician who made the Statue of Liberty "disappear" some years ago? He placed his audience and all cameras for the show on a stage he constructed facing the statue. He then closed the curtains, cutting off the view from the audience and the cameras. At the end of the show he opened the curtains to reveal that the statue was gone! In reality, the stage he constructed was an extremely slow-moving platform with special gearing that did not allow for any vibration to be felt by any one on the stage. After all "small" illusions had been performed, the "big lie" was revealed. The statue had not really moved, just those he wanted to trick.

Does the Bible say anything about "magic"? In fact, it does. The Hebrew Scriptures tell of a witch whom King Saul contacted for the purpose of conjuring up the deceased prophet Samuel (1 Samuel 28:7.) She is shocked and surprised when Samuel actually appeared because she relied on a familiar spirit. Familiar spirits are angels that rebelled against God and work to deceive human beings. They do so by imitating, both in voice, appearance, and with "secret" factual knowledge of humans who have died. When God permitted Samuel to appear, the medium was terrified because she knew it was **not** a trick!

There is also the case of Simon, user of magical arts, in Acts 8:9. It is recorded that he believed what Philip had preached to the Samaritans, but when he saw the Holy Spirit fall upon the Samaritans when Peter and John laid hands on them, he wanted to purchase the ability to perform this gift. The Bible does not say that the Holy Spirit fell on Simon. Peter's statement about perishing seems to indicate that Simon's belief was intellectual and not spiritual. There is no room for "magic" in the life of a believer.

Do Not Be Deceived

Now, what do secrets, magic, magical thinking, and being spiritually awake have to do with each other? I want you to go back to Matthew 24:24 and ask yourself why Jesus warns believers about being deceived. I have heard preachers refer to this passage out of context saying that it is about not believing false Christs during the last 2000 years. Jesus, however, is answering the disciples questions about the end of days. Clearly, *false* Christs and *false* prophets become a problem as we approach the *real* Christ's return.

It is the great signs and wonders that are intended to deceive the elect. Who are the elect? The elect are those God has chosen to save. Not every person in a church is actually born again. Not every person born of the household of Israel will enter Heaven (Romans 9:6.) Jesus wants the elect to know that there will be some very convincing sights and sounds that **could** even **deceive** (Satan's primary trick) those of us who are saved.

What does Jesus particularly stress to us? He warns us that if we are told that Christ is in the desert, **do not go to see!** It is my belief that there is a danger tied to this warning. Jesus gives us a glimpse of what His real return will be like. It will be sudden and without warning, and we will have no time to react or go anywhere. **He** will do the gathering up of His elect. One danger is in not believing what **He has told** us beforehand. Another danger lay in **why** someone would try to deceive the elect.

71

Putting the Puzzle Together

Puzzle piece A–Project Blue Beam.[4] This government project appears to rely on a mixture of electrical and natural forces, combined with satellite projection and theories put forward by Tesla to generate very convincing hologram images.[5] The proof of this program has been seen in recent years with various optical phenomena viewed by millions the world over in the sky.

On March 8th, 2009, a brilliant white figure of Jesus on the cross was seen in the sky in Russia.[6] On the night of December 9, 2009, the Norwegian spiral anomaly was photographed from northern Norway and Sweden. A *blue beam* appeared to come from behind a mountain, stop in the middle of the sky, and form a spiral of light emanating into the dark. The apparition lasted between two and three minutes.[7]

4 http://educate-yourself.org/cn/projectbluebeam25jul05.shtml
5 *Effects of GHz radiation on the human nervous system: Recent developments in the technology of political control* Analysis on Mind Control Electromagnetic Weapons. Harlan E. Girard. globalresearch.ca/globalresearch.org, May 6, 2006. NATO Advanced Research Workshop on Coherent and Emergent Phenomena in Biomolecular Systems, University of Arizona 15 January 1991.
6 Project Blue Beam: Jesus On the Cross in Russia1. verumet-inventa.wordpress.com. April 29, 2014.
7 Anyone for some Arctic roll? Mystery as spiral blue light display hovers above Norway. Mail Foreign Service. www.dailymail.co.uk. December 10, 2009.

A similar scene appeared the month before in the same area. Another example was published by *WorldNetDaily* where a pair of towering figures, appearing to wear varying hues of red and white robes, were photographed in the sky at the A5 highway near Walensee, Switzerland, their hands in a position of prayer.[8] On March 11th, 2014, a somewhat ill-defined Buddha appeared in the sky over Vietnam.[9]

It had been my desire to publish these photos in this book, but I was unable to receive permission from the sources in a timely fashion. A news article datelined Fairbanks, AK states that HAARP, or High Frequency Active Auroral Research Program, will be shut down after a final experiment takes place the middle of June, 2014. The program, established in 1993, is located in Gakonka, Alaska, and has been used for injecting energy into the ionosphere for various purposes. There are 180 antennas on the thirty-acre site. This indicates that whatever beta-testing the Air Force was doing has been completed. It has been said that part of the reason for the site has been to test some of Tesla's theories on weather, energy, and

8 Google Photo: Jesus Just Spotted In Sky? World Net Daily. Joe Kovacs. October 29, 2013.
9 Buddha appears in the sky in Vietnam. www.godlikeproductions.com/forum1/message2504123/pg1. May 11, 2014.

electricity.[10]   Can super-sized holograms be projected? **Puzzle Piece B** is a report from January 28th, 2014 that Prime Minister Recep Tayyip Erdogan of Turkey sent a giant hologram of himself speaking to a rally of supporters, blaming the reports of a banking scandal on dark groups in the government.[11] When a head of state begins to use holograms, one must ask, "For what purpose?" A talking giant would certainly be intimidating.

Speaking of sounds and speeches, it would be necessary to test whether such fear-producing sights can be heard. **Puzzle Piece C**–ELF is a program long-used by the Navies of the world to communicate with their submarine forces. ELF is Extra Low Frequency and has been blamed by many Marine Biologists for the beachings and deaths of countless dolphin and whales over the years.[12] While "scientists" have claimed that their "studies" are progressive and for the betterment

10 Air Force prepares to dismantle HAARP ahead of summer shutdown. Dermot Cole. alaskadispatch.com. May 14, 2014.

11 Turkish prime minister delivers speech as a 10 foot hologram: Recep Tayyip Erdogan addresses party faithful in a recorded green-screen message. dailymail.co.uk. Kieran Corcoran. January 28, 2014.

12 Navy Admits hundreds of dolphins will die as a result of underwater explosive training over the next five years...but they don't plan to do anything about it. AP Reporter. dailymail.co.uk/news. August 31, 2013.

of society, one must ask how these destructive inventions better anyone.

Sounds in the sky have been reported by millions around the world in recent years. The Borneo Post reported a "sky roar" over Kota Samarahan from 2 AM until 3 AM on two successive days in January, 2012. The noises were described by terrified residents as loud hushes.[13] On August 29th, 2013 at 7:30 AM in Terrace, British Columbia, Canada sounds were heard by residents that had begun in June. One resident said it sounded like a bad melody and recorded the sound for over 10 minutes.[14] In Chicago, New York, Philadelphia, Arizona, Texas, Budapest, France and Norway, metallic and almost musical sounds were heard during 2012.[15] Some news channels carried reports of clanging, disturbing noises from around the world. Notably, one report covered sounds in Germany that were loud enough to set off car alarms.

13 Sounds of mystery from the skies.www.theborneopost.com. October 28, 2012.

14 Strange Sounds Heard in Terrace, British Columbia, May Be Connected To Worldwide Phenomenon (VIDEO).www.huffingtonpost.com/2013. August 30, 2013.

15 Are These Strange Sounds Heard in the Sky Worldwide Real or a Hoax? (VIDEO). Kathy Landin. www.huffingtonpost.com. February 3, 2012.

Some who recorded the sounds said it sounded like a trumpet being blown.[16]

So far the puzzle pieces are holograms, images in the sky, and sounds heard by millions. **This is a possible answer as to why Christ would warn against going into the desert to find Him.** Camp Hero, or Montauk Air Force Station was deeded over to the New York State Park program in 1984. As late as 1994, Cardion (Siemens) Corporation had what was reported to be a particle beam radar unit in operation on the bluffs of this part of Long Island. The surface of the "park" is restricted to the public. The federal government still retains the property below the surface. The electrical meter at the "park" is marked to measure energy in the Gigawatt range–which is enough to power a city.[17]

According to researchers, the experiments at Montauk are connected to the Philadelphia Experiment reported by many newspapers and magazines in the late 1930s. Tesla and Einstein, among others, were involved in projects dealing with invisibility and

---

16 What's causing the mysterious sounds coming from the sky that are so loud they set off car alarms? Ted Thornhill. dailymail.co.uk/news. March 5, 2012.

17 Montauk Air Force Station, Active or Not? www.bibliotecapleyades.net/montauk/esp_montauk_5a.htm

teleporting large objects, even involving a Navy ship, adding even further pieces to the puzzle.[18]

Taken together, and I do not believe this to be an example of magical thinking, one may see a world-wide beta test to cause people to think that:

1) Jesus or some other religious figure has come.

2) He has called His faithful to a remote area.

3) He has come to gather them to Himself.

But remember, **do not go!** Jesus has "told you before."

---

18 The Philadelphia Experiment–The Forbidden Knowledge. www.theforbiddenknowledge.com/

EPILOGUE

He hath made everything beautiful in his time: also he hath set the world in their heart, so that no man can find out the work that God maketh from the beginning to the end. (Ecclesiastes 3:11)

Better is the end of a thing than the beginning thereof: and the patient in spirit is better than the proud in spirit. (Ecclesiastes 7:8)

Have ye not known? have ye not heard? hath it not been told you from the beginning? have ye not understood from the foundations of the earth? (Isaiah 40:21)

Who hath declared from the beginning, that we may know? and beforetime, that we may say, He is righteous? yea, there is none that sheweth, yea, there is none that declareth, yea, there is none that heareth your words. (Isaiah 41:26)

Remember the former things of old: for I am God, and there is none else; I am God, and there is none like me, [10] Declaring the end from the beginning, and from ancient times the things that are not yet done, saying, My counsel shall stand, and I will do all my pleasure. (Isaiah 46:9-10)

And now I have told you before it come to pass, that, when it is come to pass, ye might believe. (John 14:29)

I am Alpha and Omega, the beginning and the ending, saith the Lord, which is, and which was, and which is to come, the Almighty. (Revelation 1:8)

Father, Son and Holy Spirit–Three persons in One Godhead. He had no beginning. He has no end. He wants to share His "no end" with you and me. He clearly wants to share more than that. He wants to share Himself with you and me. Why else would He say in Jeremiah 3:14, "Turn, O backsliding children, saith the LORD; for I am married unto you: and I will take you one of a city, and two of a family, and I will bring you to Zion."

Father God viewed His relationship with Israel as a marriage. Interestingly, Messiah Jesus sees His wife as the Church. When you actually, deeply love someone you will be committed to them. Our God made a contract with us. He "cut a covenant" with Abraham in Genesis 15:17 that was wholly dependent on God. Christ also cut a covenant with His own blood on Calvary that accomplished the redemption of mankind and the defeat of the enemy.

Anyone who so deeply loves as our God does would also warn those whom He loves. In this small book, I have tried to put together the many warnings God has issued to the Church. It is my hope that a church somewhere might be awakened from her sleep.

Why do you think God gives warnings about future events?

First, He does not desire that any should perish (2 Peter 3:9).

Second, He deeply loves Israel and the Church.

Third, in Isaiah 41, God says that by telling us what will happen beforehand He demonstrates that He, alone, is God. There is none other. He also demonstrates that He is righteous. He wants you and me to be righteous, too.

I have studied the religions of the world for many years. They teach many things, but they do not tell what will happen in the future. There is a very prominent reason for their not forecasting coming events. They do not know what is coming. Only God knows what He is going to do (Isaiah 46). God speaks only through His Word.

We, the church have been foreordained to become like Christ.

"For whom he did foreknow, he also did predestinate *to be* conformed to the image of his Son, that he might be the firstborn among many brethren" (Romans 8:29). In order for you to become like Christ, you must be awake. It is my prayer that if you were not before, you are now.

CPSIA information can be obtained at www.ICGtesting.com
Printed in the USA
BVOW07s1100251114

376584BV00001BA/4/P

9 781498 409858